A Whale Can Wave

By Liza Charlesworth

ISBN: 978-1-339-02776-0

Art Director: Tannaz Fassihi; Designer: Tanya Chernyak
Photos © Getty Images and Shutterstock.com.

1 2 3 4 5 6 7 8 9 10   68   32 31 30 29 28 27 26 25 24 23

Printed in Jiaxing, China. First printing, August 2023.

■ SCHOLASTIC

It is a whale!
A whale can jump up.
A whale can wave its fins.

You will not spot whales
in a cage or a lake.
Whales swim in the sea!

van

A whale and a fish
are not the same thing.
Whales are big, big, big!
They can be as big as 50 vans.

A whale is brave!
It can flip and dive.

A whale can take trips.
It can swim in a cave.

Whales play fun games.
Whales chase whales!
They like to race.

krill

Munch, crunch, gulp!
Whales hunt fish and krill.
They do not like plants.

Can you spot the man?
He came to see the whale.
A man and a whale can be pals!